WHERE WE LIVE

WE LIVE IN A STATE

by Jennifer Boothroyd

Consultant: Beth Gambro
Reading Specialist, Yorkville, Illinois

Minneapolis, Minnesota

Teaching Tips

Before Reading

- Look at the cover of the book. Discuss the picture and the title.
- Ask readers to brainstorm a list of what they already know about states. What can they expect to see in the book?
- Go on a picture walk, looking through the pictures to discuss vocabulary and make predictions about the text.

During Reading

- Read for purpose. Encourage readers to think about the state they live in as they are reading.
- Ask readers to look for the details of the book. What are they learning about the things people in a state have in common?
- If readers encounter an unknown word, ask them to look at the sounds in the word. Then, ask them to look at the rest of the page. Are there any clues to help them understand?

After Reading

- Encourage readers to pick a buddy and reread the book together.
- Ask readers to name two things they might see in a state. Find the pages that tell about these things.
- Ask readers to write or draw something they learned about living in a state.

Credits:
Cover and title page, © Sundry Photography/Shutterstock; 3, © Katherine Welles/Shutterstock; 5, © Joseph Sohm/Shutterstock; 6–7, © LeoPatrizi/iStock; 9, © RLT_Images/iStock; 10, © Ron and Patty Thomas/iStock; 11, © Steve Quinlan/Shutterstock; 12–13, © Rawpixel.com/Shutterstock; 15, © lev radin/Shutterstock; 16–17, © AnaLysiSStudiO/Shutterstock; 18, © Anna39/iStock; 19, © doble-d/iStock; 20–21, © digitalskillet/iStock; 22T, © Fourleaflover/iStock; 22M, © ferrantraite/iStock, © RiverNorthPhotography/iStock; 22B, © melissamn/Shutterstock; 23TL, © Caiaimage/RobertDaly/iStock; 23TM, © pingebat/Shutterstock; 23TR, © Gregory Clifford/iStock; 23BL, © inhauscreative/iStock; 23BM, © littlenySTOCK/Shutterstock; 23BR, © Gary Gray/iStock.

Library of Congress Cataloging-in-Publication Data

Names: Boothroyd, Jennifer, 1972- author.
Title: We live in a state / by Jennifer Boothroyd.
Description: Bearcub Books. | Minneapolis, Minnesota : Bearport Publishing
   Company, [2023] | Series: Where we live | "Consultant: Beth Gambro,
   Reading Specialist, Yorkville, Illinois." | Includes bibliographical
   references and index.
Identifiers: LCCN 2023005331 (print) | LCCN 2023005332 (ebook) | ISBN
   9798888220610 (library binding) | ISBN 9798888222584 (paperback) | ISBN
   9798888223765 (ebook)
Subjects: LCSH: U.S. states--Juvenile literature.
Classification: LCC E180 .B668 2023 (print) | LCC E180 (ebook) | DDC
   973--dc23/eng/20230216
LC record available at https://lccn.loc.gov/2023005331
LC ebook record available at https://lccn.loc.gov/2023005332

Copyright © 2024 Bearport Publishing Company. All rights reserved. No part of this publication may be reproduced in whole or in part, stored in any retrieval system, or transmitted in any form or by any means, electronic, mechanical, photocopying, recording, or otherwise, without written permission from the publisher.

For more information, write to Bearport Publishing, 5357 Penn Avenue South, Minneapolis, MN 55419.

Contents

From State to State 4

State Facts 22

Glossary 23

Index 24

Read More 24

Learn More Online 24

About the Author 24

From State to State

We are going to visit Grandma.

She lives far away.

As we drive, we pass a big sign.

Now, we are in a new state!

A state is an area of land.

It is a place where many people live.

We learn and work in our state, too.

Each state is part of a larger **country**.

The United States of America is a big country.

It has 50 states.

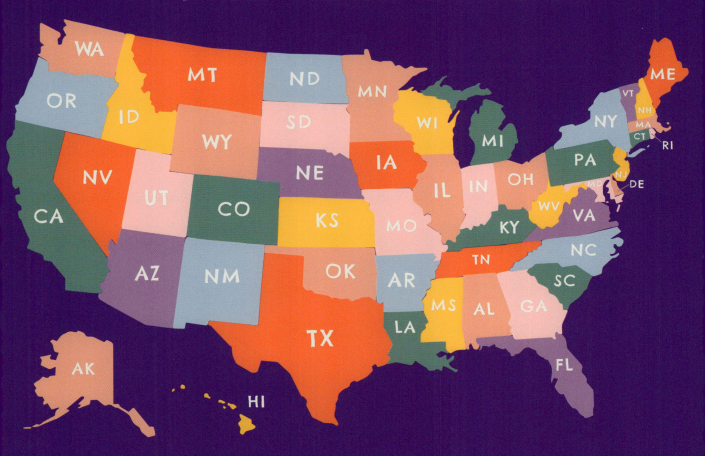

Every state is a little different.

States come in all shapes and sizes.

Ours has lakes and rivers.

Grandma lives in a state with **mountains**.

Millions of people live in some states.

Our state has a lot fewer.

No matter the size, each state has a **community** of people.

The **governor** leads the state community.

Other state workers make **laws**.

These are rules we all follow.

They keep everyone safe.

We can all help out in our state.

How can we care for other people in our state?

Treat everyone with kindness.

We can help the state's plants and animals, too.

Give them space to live.

Pick up trash and keep our waters clean.

We are all part of our state.

And we can all make our state a super place.

Our state is great!

Will you come to visit?

State Facts

There are 14 countries in the world that have states. Others break up their land in different ways.

California is the U.S. state with the most people. Wyoming has the least.

Many states celebrate what makes their state great. Some have state **fairs** where people come together.

Glossary

community a group of people that lives together or shares something in common

country a large area of land that has borders and rules for all the people who live there

fairs large gatherings with games, rides, and things to see

governor a person who leads a state

laws rules that people in a place must follow

mountains areas of land that rise very high above the land around them

Index

- **animals** 18
- **community** 12, 14
- **country** 8
- **governor** 14
- **laws** 14
- **people** 7, 12, 17, 22
- **plants** 18
- **United States of America** 8–9

Read More

Gaertner, Meg. *My State (Where I Live).* Lake Elmo, MN: Focus Readers, 2021.

Rodriguez, Alicia. *State (Where Do I Live?).* New York: Crabtree Publishing Company, 2022.

Learn More Online

1. Go to **www.factsurfer.com** or scan the QR code below.
2. Enter "**In a State**" into the search box.
3. Click on the cover of this book to see a list of websites.

About the Author

Jenny Boothroyd has lived in Illinois and Minnesota. She has been to 33 states in the United States.